# EBAY SHIPPING MADE EASY!

By Ann Eckhart

# TABLE OF CONTENTS

# INTRODUCTION

I have been selling on Ebay since 2005, and I am both a Power Seller and a Top-Rated Seller on the popular e-commerce site (the third-largest shopping site behind Amazon and Wal-mart). I have sold everything from new gift items that I ordered wholesale to secondhand treasures that I picked up at estate sales, and I have shipped out all shapes, sizes, and weights of items, from small books to heavy typewriters, to nearly every corner of the globe. I have shipped packages via the Post Office and UPS, and I have over 10,000 feedback on Ebay (not bad considering only 20-30% of Ebay customers leave sellers feedback). While Ebay has primarily been the main site I have sold on since 2005, I have also periodically sold on Amazon, Etsy, and Poshmark; and have shipped thousands of online orders from those sites, too.

In addition to selling on Ebay myself, I also teach others how to sell on Ebay via instructional videos on my YouTube channels (the links to my two YouTube channels are at the back of this book) as well as through books such as this one (the link to my Amazon Author Page for all my titles is also at the back of this book). I have covered every reselling topic under the sun, from where to source items for resale to how to handle customer service issues and everything in between.

However, despite all the instructional content I have produced over the years, the most frequently asked questions I still get from new Ebay sellers (and even some more experienced Ebay users) is: "How do I ship the items I sell on Ebay?"

Shipping is a huge part of selling online, and it is often the most overwhelming and confusing part of the Ebay process. I have seen many people not even start selling on Ebay because they are so fearful of the shipping process. Which, if you have never done it before, can seem like an impossible task.

However, there is no reason to fear shipping out orders as Ebay makes it incredibly EASY to print labels directly from their site. In this book, I will show you how EASY and COST-EFFECTIVE it is to ship your items through Ebay, including the step-by-step processes for setting up shipping within your listings as well as the step-by-step processes for printing out labels.

If you have been taking your Ebay packages directly to the Post Office to have the postage calculated, this book will save you an enormous amount of time and money as you will be able to print labels from the comfort of your own home and, if you want, even arrange for your postal carrier to pick them up from your home. After reading this book, I promise that you will kick yourself for ever taking your packages to the Post Office for postage! In fact, the only time I ever take my own packages to the Post Office is if my internet has gone out and I cannot access Ebay from my computer. And even then, I will sometimes delay shipping until my internet comes back on as it is just so much easier to print my own labels.

While there are many different shipping carriers and dozens of package options available to ship out the items you sell on Ebay, in this book, I am going to focus on shipping packages within the United States of America (although I will briefly touch on international shipping, too) using the United States Postal Service (USPS). Again, this book is about making the shipping process as easy as possible for you; so, I will be giving you the essential information you need to start shipping your own orders out immediately.

In this book, I will be focusing on the four main ways you can ship out the orders you sell on Ebay via USPS:

- **Media Mail**
- **First Class Mail**
- **Parcel Select**
- **Priority Mail**

Note that there are many other options available for shipping via the Post Office, including Express and overnight services, but the vast majority of Ebay shipping is done through USPS via the four methods above. Thus, there is no need to worry about any other services aside from these four for those just starting out. In fact, I rarely use any other methods to ship my Ebay orders. Once in a great while, I will ship a large, heavy package via UPS Ground, but 99.9% of all my orders ship out via the Post Office. And in my fifteen years of reselling, I have only ever sent one package via an overnight service.

Shipping out the items you sell on Ebay involves more than just purchasing postage, however. Actually, printing the shipping label is the EASIEST part of the process. Before you print a label, you need to have the supplies on hand to know HOW you are going to ship your items (in a box or envelope and via what service); and you need to understand how to set up your Ebay listing so that your customers are paying the right amount of postage. If you are just starting out, all these steps can seem overwhelming; however, I will show you how EASY it all really is in this book. And once you have mastered the basics of shipping, you will be able to carry that knowledge with you as you continue to sell online, perhaps even expanding onto other sites such as Poshmark or Etsy.

I have seen many new Ebay sellers so confused about shipping that they take all their packages to be weighed at the Post Office and for the clerks there to print the shipping labels. Not only is this a massive waste of time, but it is more expensive than printing your own postage from home. Why? Well, purchasing package postage at the Post Office counters is more expensive than buying that same postage online. USPS offers discounted package postage rates when you buy and print labels directly from the USPS website. But when you ship your packages directly through Ebay, you get that online discount and other discounts exclusive to Ebay. These postage discounts increase based on your seller's performance. So, printing out your own postage really does save you loads of time, but it also saves you a lot of money!

Of all the things you do to sell on Ebay (sourcing products, taking photos, creating listings, answering customer questions), creating an Ebay shipment should be the EASIEST part of the process. And that is where this book comes in.

There is no need to waste time and money hauling your packages to the Post Office to have them weigh your packages and print your postage for you. If you follow the steps offered in this book, you will be shipping our Ebay orders from your own home quickly and easily in less time than it took you to read this introduction!

There are four sections that I will cover in this book:

- **Part One: Shipping Supplies**
- **Part Two: Package Categories**
- **Part Three: How To Set Up The Shipping In An Ebay Listing**
- **Part Four: Printing Shipping Labels Through Ebay**

Now, just because there are only four sections in this book does not mean that each is not JAM-PACKED with valuable information! My goal with this book is to provide you everything you need to know in an easy-to-understand format. I cut through all the chit-chat and get straight to the point so that you can start shipping – and making money – quickly on Ebay!

Shipping directly through Ebay is FAST, EASY, and CHEAPER than having the postal clerks print the postage for you. So, if you are ready to learn how to ship your packages through Ebay, let's get started!

# PART ONE: SHIPPING SUPPLIES

B efore you can actually list an item on Ebay or ship it out, you need to have the proper supplies on hand. I am covering this topic first because I feel it is the most important step you need to take to ensure you are shipping your packages correctly and for the best possible rate. Shipping out Ebay orders involves more than just purchasing postage; there are supplies that you also need to have to ensure that your orders are processed as efficiently and professionally as possible.

**Computer, Internet & Printer:** If you are going to sell on Ebay, you obviously need a computer with an internet connection. A reliable computer with a fast process that is connected to high-speed internet is worth the investment, especially when it comes to printing out shipping labels.

If you want to really make good money on Ebay but are using an outdated, sluggish computer, it is time to invest in an updated model. I typically buy my computers at Sam's Club. I look for models that go on clearance, which frequently happens as new systems are continually being released. For Ebay, the essential feature of a computer is that it has a fast processor, which makes listing and printing shipping labels go much faster. I also look for models that have a comfortable keyboard and a nice sized screen. Costco is another warehouse club that also frequently has good deals on computers. But if you need more assistance in choosing a new system, Best Buy and any of the office supply stores have associates that can assist you in person.

Of course, you cannot access Ebay without internet access. It is always worth a phone call to your local internet provider to see if they have any special offers on upgraded internet service. I recently upgraded to a higher speed of broadband and was given a discount for switching my plans; so, I am currently paying less for better internet speed than I was previously.

The most significant benefit of shipping your packages from your own home or office is the cost savings, but if you are going to print your own postage, you, of course, also need a printer. What type of printer you choose, one that uses ink/toner or one that prints via thermal imaging, is up to you.

I use a LaserJet printer that prints in black and white for my Ebay shipping labels. The model I use is fast, it prints numerous pages from one toner cartridge, and it fits squarely in a corner on my desk. While one toner cartridge costs about $70, I only need to purchase one, maybe two, a year. I print my Ebay shipping labels out onto peel-and-stick label sheets. These sheets feature two labels each. I print out a label for one order and then flip the sheet around to print a second order label.

If you are just starting to sell on Ebay and already have a printer, use it until you see a need to upgrade to a better model. Note that if you are using an inkjet (versus a LaserJet) printer that it uses a lot of expensive ink and you must change the cartridges frequently. Even if you are just going to be shipping out a few packages each day, you will eventually want to upgrade your printer to at least a LaserJet model. I personally bought my current printer, an HP LaserJet P1606dn, during a Black Friday sale at Staples when it was half off, paying less than $100 for it. And it has lasted me several years now.

As your Ebay sales increase, you may consider purchasing a thermal printer specifically designed for printing shipping labels. I have been selling on Ebay since 2005, and I am still fine using a LaserJet; however, you may eventually determine that a printer dedicated to solely printing shipping labels is better for your business, not just for the cost savings but also for efficiency.

Thermal printers that are specially designed to only print out shipping labels are widely recommended among resellers, not only those who sell on Ebay but also those who sell on Poshmark, Etsy, and Mercari. DYMO sells several Label Printer systems starting at $70 and going up to over $200. There are numerous other brands of thermal printers available, too. The benefit of these printers is that you do NOT need to refill them with ink or toner; they print using thermal printing technology. However, you do need to purchase specially sized labels for them. These label refills are a bit more expensive than a package of the peel-and-stick label sheets that I personally use in my LaserJet printer. But then again, I also must purchase toner cartridge refills. The price difference between using a LaserJet versus a thermal printer comes into play if you are shipping out dozens of orders every single day.

Thermal shipping label printers are extremely popular in the reselling community. As you grow your Ebay business and start interacting with other Ebay sellers online (there are large reselling communities on Facebook, Instagram, and YouTube), you will see many other sellers using them. However, again, I caution against jumping right in and purchasing one of these systems as a basic printer will handle the job of printing shipping labels just fine, even onto regular copy paper, as you begin your Ebay selling journey. If I only have one order to ship, I will print the shipping label out onto a piece of white paper, cut it out, and tape it to the box to not waste the expensive peel-and-stick labels.

Like many more advanced pieces of office equipment, thermal printers are costly and can take time to learn to use effectively. I always recommend waiting a while before investing in one to make sure it is something you will use and that it will make your business operations more effective. I ordered a thermal printer a few years back, but I ended up returning it as I personally found it easier to just ship via a standard printer. You may decide differently, but give yourself some time before deciding to switch to a thermal model.

**Ebay, PayPal, and Managed Payments:** To sell on Ebay, you used to need both an Ebay account AND a PayPal account. For years, PayPal was Ebay's payment system; it worked like a debit card for buyers. Customers created a PayPal account and connected it to their bank account and/or credit/debit card. When they purchased something on Ebay, the money was paid to the seller directly through PayPal. And for sellers, the cost of shipping labels came out of their PayPal balances.

The PayPal system eliminated the need for sellers to have their own merchant (i.e., credit card processing) accounts, and it also prevented customers and sellers from having to exchange their personal banking information with one another. Sellers could access their PayPal funds at any time, either using them to pay for their own online purchases or withdrawing the money to their bank accounts whenever they pleased.

However, in 2015, Ebay and PayPal parted ways, and Ebay began developing their own payment system, which they call Managed Payments. Managed Payments allows customers to purchase items on Ebay directly without also having to have a PayPal account. Just as buyers can use credit or debit cards directly on Amazon, they can now set up their payment preferences directly on Ebay. And while customers can still opt to use their PayPal accounts to pay for items, sellers no longer must have a PayPal account to sell on Ebay. Ebay now collects all payments and runs postage costs through the site directly, and Ebay now disperses the funds for every seller. No longer can sellers access their funds whenever they like the way they could with PayPal; Ebay now holds funds and disperses them either daily or once a week, per the seller's wishes.

The Managed Payments system also means that sellers no longer must pay for postage from their PayPal accounts; instead, the funds come directly from their pending Managed Payments balance. When a seller used PayPal, the money from every order was deposited into their PayPal account. The Ebay shipping label was also connected to their PayPal account. When a seller went onto Ebay to print a shipping label, Ebay had to connect to PayPal to pull the money to pay for the postage before the label could be printed. This entire process is now done entirely on the Ebay site.

Note that you need to keep a bank account on file with Ebay so that they can disperse any money you have earned. You can choose daily or weekly deposits (I have weekly payouts to get a more considerable lump sum once a week, almost like a weekly paycheck). Any postage costs are taken directly from your pending payments, so you do not accumulate any outstanding shipping charges.

**Digital Postage Scale:** The number one supply you MUST have if you are going to sell on Ebay is a digital postage scale to weigh packages. You can buy digital postage scales for around $20 on Ebay and Amazon, and they are also sold at office supply stores. A small unit that fits easily on your desk or on a nearby table is best so that you can weigh items as you list them and again when you go to print out a shipping label.

You do not need a fancy digital postage scale, just one explicitly designated for postage that weighs ounces and pounds. I have two postage scales, one for my office and one in my Ebay inventory room. A digital postage scale is a small investment you need to make if you are going to ship your Ebay orders yourself. If you are not willing to purchase a digital postage scale for your Ebay business, then you should stop reading this book and resign yourself to hauling all your packages to the Post Office. Or you can spend the $20 and handle shipping from the comfort of your own home.

I have encountered many sellers over the years who sell on Ebay without a digital postage scale. They estimate the shipping, overcharging customers in some cases (and getting negative feedback), or undercharging and losing money. I have even met some Ebay sellers who take all their items to the Post Office before they even list them to get a weight on each. They then haul the items back home, list them, and then take them back to the Post Office for postage after they sell. That, to me, is a HUGE waste of time and gas money! For a fraction of the time and cost, you can print out your own postage at home.

I also see many sellers charging all customers one flat rate for shipping, which can be another big mistake. Buyers come to Ebay for deals, and the shipping charges factor into that. As I stated above, charging one flat rate will result in overcharging some customers and undercharging others. Changing a flat rate can work if you sell similar items, such as jewelry or lightweight clothing. But even then, shipping weights can vary widely. For instance, a heavy beaded necklace weighs more than a pair of dainty earrings. And a winter parka weighs more than a tank top. The difference between shipping a four-ounce item versus a two-pound item can be as much as eight dollars within the United States.

However, if you offer *Calculated Shipping*, the buyer pays the actual shipping cost based on the package's weight and the zip code it is going to. If you have a digital postage scale on hand, using calculated shipping is a breeze. I will talk more about calculated shipping later in this book

Some sellers, such as myself, offer "free" shipping, padding the postage cost into the price of the item. While offering free shipping is a smart move for lightweight items (for instance, if you have a piece of jewelry that weighs 2-ounces, you can easily offer free shipping and absorb the $3 it will cost to ship), it can backfire on heavier items as buyers know when a seller has inflated the price of an item to cover shipping. You do not want to give the appearance that you are making money from the shipping costs and risk getting negative feedback from a disgruntled buyer. I tend to offer "free shipping" on items that weigh less than one pound as those orders ship via First Class, and I can add the postage cost to the item's price. And having a digital postage scale makes knowing that easy.

Instead of guessing the postage costs or running back and forth to the Post Office, you can save time and money by quickly printing your shipping labels from home....and a digital postage scale makes that possible!

**Boxes & Envelopes:** Having an Ebay business means you will likely accumulate as much in shipping materials as you do in inventory. After all, you cannot just stick a label directly on a book and send it in the mail (although I have unfortunately seen this happen). Shipping out Ebay orders requires that you keep all manner of shipping supplies on hand, specifically boxes and envelopes.

The great thing about the United States Postal Service (USPS) is that they offer FREE Priority Mail shipping boxes (I will be talking a lot more about Priority Mail and their various forms of shipping services later in this book). And while Priority Mail is an excellent option for shipping many packages, you will need other forms of packaging for Media Mail, First Class Mail, and Parcel Select, as well as for international shipments (again, more on these forms of shipping coming up). Basically, you need two types of shipping boxes/envelopes: USPS Priority Mail boxes and envelopes, and plain boxes and envelopes for the order that ship via Media, First Class, and Parcel.

Before you run out and buy a bunch of new shipping boxes and envelopes, check around your house to see what you have on hand. Plain cardboard boxes, manila envelopes, and bubble mailers can all be used for non-Priority mail. If you already have items on hand that you will be listing on Ebay, look them over to determine the packaging they will need. Perhaps you are only going to sell books, for which bubble mailers and sturdy boxes are enough. If you are only selling clothing, you will need lots of poly bag mailers as well as some Flat Rate boxes for heavier items such as shoes. However, if you only plan to sell hard goods, you do not need to worry about stocking up on envelopes or poly mailers, just various sizes of boxes.

I keep a wide variety of boxes and envelopes on hand. While I utilize the free Priority Mail boxes and bubble mailers from the Post Office, I also invest in nice shipping boxes and poly mailer envelopes from Ebay, Amazon, Sam's Club, and companies such as Uline and ValueMailers. I also save any quality shipping boxes I myself receive from personal orders from sites such as Amazon.

Here is a list of the types of shipping boxes and envelopes I personally keep on hand for my Ebay business:

**Standard Priority Mail Boxes:**

- **Priority Mail Shoe Box:** Not only great for shoes but also helpful for shipping dolls and other tall items such as candlesticks.
- **Priority Mail Box #4 7x7x6-inch:** This is the perfect size box for shipping figurines, coffee mugs, and ornaments.
- **Priority Mail Box #7 12x12x8-inch:** I use this box frequently as it holds larger items or several smaller items. I can typically ship this size for less than the Flat Rate version.
- **Priority Mail Rectangular Boxes:** USPS offers a few sizes of flat rectangle boxes (12x15x3, 11x13x2, 9x6x3). I only keep a handful of each size in my supply, but they do come in handy for bulky clothing and some toys such as smaller games and puzzles.

**Flat Rate Priority:**

- **Priority Mail Padded Flat Rate Envelope:** These are a favorite among resellers as you can stuff heavier pieces of clothing inside and ship for a cheaper rate than if you used a regular box. A tip for stuffing items into these envelopes is to first put the item into a clear non-suffocation polybag; it will then slid easily into the bubble mailer while also adding an extra layer of protection for the item.

- **Priority Mail Small Flat Rate Box:** The perfect size for shipping heavy jewelry or several small items together, such as belt buckles or other small metal objects.
- **Priority Mail Medium Flat Rate Box:** There are two sizes of the Medium Flat Rate boxes, a flat rectangle and a fuller rectangle size; I like to keep both sizes on hand.
- **Priority Mail Large Flat Rate Box:** I only keep a few of this size box on hand. I can usually ship items cheaper via regular Priority or in a Regional Rate box, but this size is nice if you have a small yet very heavy item.
- **Priority Mail Regional Rate Boxes A1 & A2:** These boxes ship at a rate based on the buyer's zip code and, for me, are often cheaper to ship than the regular Flat Rate options.
- **Priority Mail Regional Rate Boxes B1 & B2**: Depending on your location, the B options of these Regional Rate Boxes may be cheaper than the A versions. Since I am centrally located in Iowa, the A boxes are the best price for me, so I personally do not keep any B boxes on hand.

Note that the Post Office also offers other free Priority Mail boxes and envelopes, including a large Flat Rate Game Board (which often costs much more to ship than if you craft your own box), Tubes (for rolled posters and artwork), and Express. However, the envelopes and boxes I listed above are the only ones I use and are the ones most resellers keep on hand. You can order any of the USPS shipping boxes and envelopes for FREE, and your postal carrier will even deliver them to you for FREE, too!

**Plain Cardboard Boxes:**

Since I sell a wide variety of items, from clothing and books to figurines and toys, I need to keep several different sizes of boxes on hand. And while I prefer to use the Priority Mail boxes that I get for free from the Post Office, for shipping orders via First Class, Media Mail, or Parcel select, I need plain boxes. It depends on what you sell for what sizes you will need, but I keep lots of square options (6x6x6, 8x8x8, 10x10x10, and 12x12x12) on hand at all times. I have also invested in some flatter options, such as 10x10x2 for shipping heavy books.

Note that to ship via USPS Priority Mail, boxes can be no larger than 12x12x12. I keep a small number of 14x14x14 and 16x16x16 boxes in my supply for oversized orders that I ship via Parcel Select. However, the cost to ship these larger sizes is much higher, hence why I stick to smaller items to resell.

If you are just starting out selling on Ebay, try to use any boxes you have on hand first before ordering any; and don't be shy about asking your friends and family for any boxes they may have. With more and more people shopping online, many people have accumulated cardboard boxes they are desperate to get rid of.

If you are using repurposed boxes, be sure to use a marker to black out any writing on the outside of the box, specifically any barcodes. You want to neatly cover up any company names or other information on the outside of the box that may interfere with the box being scanned at the Post Office. I always pick up the thick black Sharpies when I see them for cheap for this very purpose. We also use Ebay stickers to cover up the writing on boxes.

Also, do not wrap your shipping boxes in brown paper. This is something I see a lot of new Ebay sellers do, but it is entirely unnecessary. Not only is it a waste of time and money, the Post Office actually prefers that you do NOT wrap your boxes as the paper can become lodged in the sorting machines.

**Poly & Bubble Mailers:**

Plastic poly shipping bags and bubble mailers are staples in most Ebay seller's shipping supply stockpiles. However, if you are only selling hard goods such as ceramics, glassware, figurines, and toys, you likely will not need to keep these types of bags on hand. However, if you sell clothing, books, and/or stuffed animals, they are ideal for shipping as they are much lighter than boxes. And the lighter the packaging you use is, the less postage will cost.

If you do decide to stock poly bags and bubble mailers, the 8x10 and 9x12 sizes are the most popular. If you plan to ship large parka coats and/or oversized plush toys, then you may want to stock larger sizes. Of course, the USPS Priority Flat Rate Bubble Mailers is THE preferred shipping envelope for most resellers as it ships anything over one-pound for one low flat rate. For instance, it costs me over ten dollars to ship a two-pound sweater to California. But if I put that same sweater in a Flat Rate Bubble mailer, the price drops to $8.15 when I print the label directly from the Ebay site (if I were to take the same envelope to the Post Office, they would charge me $8.50 for postage).

## Ebay Branded Shipping Supplies:

Ebay has a store dedicated to branded shipping supplies. One benefit of having an Ebay store of Basic or higher is that Ebay will give you a quarter shipping supply coupon (actually, it is more like a gift card) that you can spend on these supplies. The amount of the coupon depends on your store level.

- **Basic Ebay Store:** $21.95 a month when you commit to a year-long subscription. Basic Store subscribers receive a $25 shipping supply coupon every quarter.
- **Premium Ebay Store:** $59.95 a month when you commit to a year-long subscription. Premium Store subscribers receive a $50 shipping supply coupon every quarter.
- **Anchor Ebay Store:** $299.95 a month when you commit to a year-long subscription. Anchor Store subscribers receive a $150 shipping supply coupon every quarter.
- **Enterprise Ebay Store:** $2,999.95 per month when you commit to a year-long subscription. Enterprise Store subscribers receive a $150 shipping supply coupon every quarter.

Note that there is also a Basic Store subscription level, but that level does not include the shipping supply coupon. So, if you are thinking about opening a store but cannot decide between the Basic or Starter level, the fact that you will get $100 during the year ($25 in January, April, July, and October) is a benefit to consider.

If you have a qualifying store subscription level, Ebay will provide you with a unique code every quarter to apply to the branded shipping supplies in their store. Note that you can also purchase these items any time during the year without the coupon. All these supplies ship for free, too. The selection includes:

- **Mailjacket Envelopes**
- **Padded Mailers**
- **Poly Mailers**
- **Shipping Boxes**
- **Thank You Cards**
- **Shipping Tape**
- **Stickers**
- **Tissue Paper**

There are several size options for each of the envelopes, mailers, and boxes. Over the years, I have tried to use my coupon for each size to have a wide selection on hand. I also like to use my coupons for the shipping tape and tissue paper. And I also grab the stickers as they are useful when needing to cover up writing outside of repurposed boxes.

It is essential that you use your entire Ebay shipping coupon every quarter, even if you go over your allotted amount and end up paying a bit out of pocket. This is because you can only use your coupon ONCE; if you do not use it all in one go, you will lose any money you did not use. I'd rather pay a few dollars out of pocket than lose any unused shipping credit.

To find your Ebay shipping supply coupon, simply visit your **Seller Hub** and click on the **Marketing** tab. From the drop-down menu, select **Subscriber Discounts.** The first box you will see on the next page is for your **Ebay Shipping Supplies.** Simply click on **See details,** and you will be directed to a page with your unique code. Copy the code and enter it into the coupon field when you check out. You can usually expect to receive your order in under a week.

Shipping supplies are definitely an investment in your business. Of course, what you need depends on what you sell. Remember that you can claim any supplies you use in your Ebay business as an expense come tax time, so be sure to keep an accurate record of anything you purchase for your business.

**Packing Materials:** You cannot just throw an item into a box and ship it as is (well, you CAN, as I have seen some sellers do; but you shouldn't). You need to WRAP up your items to protect them inside of their shipping box. Since I have an established Ebay business, I invest in **recycled packing paper** to wrap up my items before placing them inside their shipping box. However, I then use **packing peanuts** or crumpled **newspapers** to protect the item further. Do NOT wrap your item in the newspaper directly; you do not want any newspaper ink to bleed onto your products. Finally, I keep a supply of **tissue paper** on hand to buffer smaller items, such as figurines. I like to use tissue paper to tuck into any small crevices a piece may have to prevent breakage during shipping.

In addition to packing paper, I also purchase **bubble wrap** for shipping packages. In my area, I have found Sam's Club to have the best price on bubble wrap (you can buy it in-store or order it online). Bubble wrap is a MUST for protecting ceramics such as coffee mugs (of which I sell a lot of!), figurines, ceramics, and glassware. You can let your friends and family know that you are willing to take any bubble wrap that may have accumulated. Most people are happy to give you're their unwanted bubble wrap as it cannot be recycled.

**Packing peanuts** are always nice to have on hand to use in shipments, but buying them new is expensive. I save any that I get from online orders I myself place, and, as with bubble wrap, I let my friends and family know that I will gladly take their unwanted packing peanuts off their hands. Most people are happy to get rid of the packing peanuts they have as they are a static mess to deal with. Otherwise, I buy packing peanuts in bulk from Amazon.

Another source of free bubble wrap and packing peanuts are locally-owned shops, especially gift stores. I know several resellers who have developed relationships with local business owners who are stuck with packing materials that they cannot recycle who are happy to give it to them for free.

**Finally, corrugated cardboard rolls** are perfect if you plan on shipping breakables (I buy mine on Amazon). These rolls of cardboard are used to wrap fragile items in order to provide an extra layer of protection. I call this the "box-in-a-box" method. For instance, when shipping a coffee mug, I first wrap it in bubble wrap. I then put a strip of the cardboard roll around it, making a sort of box for it. I then wrap another piece of bubble wrap around the cardboard. Finally, I use crumpled up newspaper or packing peanuts to surround the item inside of the shipping box.

While this may sound like overkill and a waste of packing materials, with the increase in online shopping, carriers are more stressed than ever with the overload of packages they must deliver each day. Boxes are thrown and dropped all day long, so it is vital that you adequately buffer items inside of the shipping box. Test your packaging strength by tossing a completed box into the air. If you hear or feel anything move, open it up and stuff in more packing materials.

**Packing Tape:** So, you now have boxes (all sizes), envelopes (both poly and bubble in multiple sizes), packing paper, newspaper, tissue paper, bubble wrap, packing peanuts, and maybe even corrugated cardboard rolls. In order to close up your packages, you need packing tape.

Clear packing tape can be found at drugstores, big-box retailers, office supply stores, warehouse clubs, and even the dollar stores. I purchase my shipping tape at Sam's Club. Dollar for dollar, I find it to be the best quality and the best price. Costco also sells shipping tape in bulk for the same price as Sam's Club, and if you do not live close to either store, you can order from them both online.

Note that you want to purchase SHIPPING tape, not packing tape. Packing tape is for moving boxes and is not as strong, while shipping tape is meant to hold packages together as they travel to their destination by vehicle, boat, and/or air.

I also have a red hand-held Mead brand tape dispenser (sold right next to the tape). If you are just starting out selling on Ebay, I recommend buying a kit with the tape dispenser and some extra tape rolls. You can usually find such kits for $10-15 in the tape section of most big-box stores. You only need to buy the dispenser once and then tape refills as needed. I have used a larger industrial size tape dispenser in the past, but I honestly like the smaller hand-held ones better for my needs.

In addition to packing tape, it is also handy to keep scotch tape at the ready. Paper clips, box cutters, scissors, and markers are also items I keep in my shipping area.

**Enclosures:** Something I strongly encourage all Ebay sellers to do is to put enclosures into their shipments. You should at least consider including a packing slip with all orders. Ebay makes it super easy to do this as after you print a label, there is a link you can click on to print a packing slip. The packing slip is just a copy of the original invoice that was sent to the customer when they purchased the item.

Since I use the shipping labels that print two to a sheet, I print out an item's shipping label, which prints on the shipping label sheet. I then click the option to print a packing slip, which prints out on a plain sheet of paper. I then take both sheets out of my printer and turn them around to print off the postage and packing slip for my second order. I then cut the sheets in half and put them in their respective packages before moving them to my packaging area, where I will wrap them, put them in their respective shipping containers, and put on the mailing labels. Once all of my packages are ready, I put them in a bag to be ready for my mail carrier to take them the following day.

I must admit that when I first started selling on Ebay, I did not want to include a packing slip as I did not want to spend the money on ink and paper. Fortunately, I was able to chat with some experienced Ebay sellers who convinced me that including a packing slip was a vital part of maintaining a professional image. I know that when I order something online, I am put off if there is not a packing slip inside. So why should I treat my Ebay customers any differently?

In addition to a packing slip, I also include enclosure cards in my shipments. Over the years, these have ranged from business cards to large postcards. No matter the size, the cards have always thanked the customer for their order and given them the direct link to my Ebay store. I order these enclosure cards from VistaPrint.com, where they allow you to create professional business materials at a great price. However, there are several online printing services available that also offer these types of promotional products; or you may choose to seek out a local company to order these types of items from.

These days, I include a packing slip and a business card sized thank you card in all my packages. The thank you card has my business logo at the top and "THANK YOU FOR YOUR ORDER" underneath. I then provide a direct link to my Ebay store. Years ago, I also gave buyers my email address to contact me if there were any issues, but I stopped adding that several years ago as Ebay now makes it easy for sellers and buyers to communicate directly through Ebay's messaging system. I want to handle all Ebay issues directly on Ebay's site, not have customers emailing me off the site when I will just have to redirect them to Ebay's system, anyway.

If you are just starting out selling on Ebay, I recommend that you include a packing slip and perhaps write "Thank You!" on it to give it a personal touch. If you decide that you want to make Ebay a part-time or even a full-time business, you can then investigate having enclosure cards printed up. Resist the urge to spend extra money on fancy thank you cards; taking the time to write a personal thank you note to every customer is nice in theory, but it takes up valuable time that you could be spending sourcing or listing.

**Shipping Station:** Now that you have all your shipping supplies, you need a place to prepare your shipments. If you have space, it is nice to designate an entire area for shipping. I have a table in my office where my digital scale always sits at the ready. It is right next to my computer to weigh items as I am listing them (again, lots more on this coming up). The most important thing is to have your digital scale on a flat surface so that you can get an accurate reading.

I have shelving for all my boxes, envelopes, packing materials, and tape. Again, since I have an established business, I have a lot of materials. However, if you are just starting out, use an out-of-the-way space (perhaps in the basement or in the corner of a spare room) for your shipping supplies. You want to make sure your supplies (and the items you are selling) are away from any smoke, pets, or other household odors. Yes, customers WILL complain if they find dog hair inside their packages; and cigarette smoke complaints can lead to negative feedback.

I have found that the large banquet-sized folding tables work great as shipping stations as you can put materials on top and underneath. Note that what you sell will determine how much room you need to dedicate to your shipping. If you only sell clothing, you will likely only stock poly mailers and maybe a handful of boxes; you also will not be using bubble wrap or packing peanuts. Therefore, you will not need nearly the same space that someone like me, who ships all sorts of items, does.

# PART TWO: PACKAGE CATEGORIES

There are dozens of carriers and ways you can ship packages. While UPS and FedEx are viable shipping options, you will want to stick with shipping the vast majority of your packages through the United States Postal Service (USPS) when you are just starting out selling on Ebay (and even as you grow your business; 99.9% of all my packages still ship out via USPS exclusively). The USPS provides the best value and service for small online sellers, and Ebay has partnered with them to make shipping easy and cost-effective. Since the USPS is Ebay's preferred shipping partner, if you sell on Ebay, you will be using them a lot.

While there are numerous ways you can ship a package through the Post Office, most Ebay sellers ship via one of four methods, all of which are for shipments within the United States (including San Juan, Puerto Rico, and military bases):

- **Media Mail**
- **First Class Mail**
- **Parcel Select**
- **Priority Mail**

**Media Mail:** Media Mail is for, surprise, MEDIA! It is preferable to ship books via *Media Mail* because they are heavy, and you get a discounted rate. However, the low price also means that *Media Mail* is extremely slow, sometimes taking up to one month (although the Post Office claims delivery is 2-8 business days).

The following items qualify to be shipped via *Media Mail*:

- Books of at least eight printed pages
- 16-millimeter or narrower width films and catalogs of films 24 pages or more
- Printed music
- Educational testing materials and printed educational materials
- Sound recordings
- Playscripts and manuscripts
- Loose-leaf pages and their binders of education medical information
- Computer-readable media

*Media Mail* can NOT be used for advertising, video games, computer drives, or digital drives. The maximum weight for a *Media Mail* package is 70-pounds.

Some sellers try to cheat the system by shipping heavy, non-media items via *Media Mail*. This is a violation of the USPS policy and can result in you losing your postal account. Post offices are notorious for opening boxes marked as *Media Mail* to make sure they only contain approved media items, so be careful to follow the rules.

**Media Mail items can only be shipped in plain boxes or envelopes**, NOT in the *Priority Mail* boxes. When you print a label via Ebay (more on how to do this coming up), it will clearly state on the label which service you paid for. So, if you print a *Media Mail* label, it will say "MEDIA MAIL" at the top.

**First Class:** *First Class mail* is the service you use when you send a postcard or letter weighing 3.5 ounces or less. While one stamp equals one ounce on a rectangular postcard or letter up to 3.5-ounces, anything 4-ounces or larger is charged at a higher PACKAGE RATE. Unless you are selling postcards or brochures that fit in standard letter envelopes, you will be paying the package rate to ship your Ebay orders.

You can ship up to 16-ounces (1-pound) via *First Class*. Like *Media Mail,* **First Class packages must be in plain boxes or envelopes;** you can NOT use the free *Priority Mail* boxes or envelopes to ship *First Class* packages.

Shipping items via *First Class* is where having a digital postal scale really comes in handy as you can get your package weight down to the exact ounce. The *First Class* cost varies by weight and zone, so it is essential to get as close a weight on your package as possible (I will talk more about weighing your packages coming up later in this book). If you are using *Calculated Shipping* and having your customers pay the shipping charge, offering them *First Class* postage saves them money. If the package you are sending weighs 8-ounces, for instance, the difference between *First Class* and *Parcel* or *Priority* can be as much as $6 depending on the location the item is shipping to.

You save a significant amount on postage when you print your labels directly through Ebay. Not only do you get a discount for shipping online, but your seller level can also mean you get an extra discount. Therefore, knowing exactly how much each package weighs will help you keep control of your postage costs.

However, even with a digital scale, finding the exact ounce can be challenging as you need an item weight before you list an item. My trick, and one that I will talk more about later in this book, is to add 3-ounces to the weight of all packages to account for packing materials. So, if you have a small item that, on its own, weighs 5-ounces, list it as 8-ounces. That way, when it is in an envelope with a packing slip, you will not risk the Post Office sending it back for insufficient postage.

Since I typically offer "free shipping" on my items, I do not have to worry about what I am charging the customer. I weigh my items before I list them so that I know how much to pad the item price to account for shipping, and I weigh them again when I ship them to get the actual postage cost. Yes, I add in the postage cost to my "free" listings as shipping is NOT "free;" someone, in this case, me, must pay for it. Buyers, however, like "free shipping," so this little trick works to not only entice customers but to avoid complaints about postage costs.

**Parcel Select:** *Parcel Select*, formerly called *Parcel Post*, is for packages weighing over 16-ounces. *Parcel* is slower than *Priority* (shipping time can take up to two weeks, although the Post Office claims 2-8 business days), but it is cheaper for heavy shipments. *Parcel* **shipments must be in plain boxes or envelopes**; just as with *Media Mail* and *First Class*, you can NOT ship *Parcel Select* shipments in the *Priority Mail* boxes. The maximum weight for *Parcel* packages is 70-pounds.

*Parcel Select* postage's cost depends on the weight of the package and where it is going to. That is why, for items over 1-pound, that it is smart to use Ebay's *Calculated Shipping* as the customer pays for the exact shipping for their zip code.

While *Parcel Select* is an excellent option for heavy packages, you want to make sure to check the cost between *Parcel* and *Priority* when you are creating your shipping label through Ebay (again, I will be going over how to do this coming up). Depending on how far away the package is going, *Priority Mail* may be the cheaper option.

For example, I am in Iowa, centrally located between both coasts in the middle of the country. For packages weighing less than four pounds, it is often cheaper for me to ship via *Priority Mail* over *Parcel Select*. Plus, I get to use a Priority free box, and I get a discount on postage by shipping directly through Ebay.

What is great about shipping through Ebay is that you can look at all the package and price options before paying for and printing a label. For me, that means I can find the best rate AND the fastest shipping time for each order. It is always nice when a customer chooses *Parcel,* but I can upgrade them to *Priority.* Not only does it save money, but the item arrives much faster. Don't worry; I will be going over how to do this later in this book.

**Priority Mail:** *Priority Mail* is for packages weighing over 16-ounces or more that need to get to their location quickly, typically 2-3 business days. Note that "business days" means weekdays and does not include Saturdays, Sundays, or federal holidays. If you ship an item out on a Friday, realize that it may not be processed and scanned at your area Post Office until Monday. From there, it will have an additional 2-3 days before it reaches the customer. Larger postal hubs may scan and process shipments on the weekends, but most do not. Regardless, Ebay stands by the 2-3 weekday shipping timeframe for all sellers.

As I explained above, when considering shipping via *Parcel Select,* sometimes *Priority Mail* may actually be the cheaper option. For me, this is often true for packages weighing less than four pounds that are going to either coast. I also get a shipping discount because I ship directly through Ebay, and I get the *Priority Mail* boxes for free. In fact, the vast majority of my shipments go via *Priority Mail* as nine times out of ten, it ends up being the cheapest option for packages between one and four pounds.

*Priority Mail* has other bonuses over *Parcel Select,* including FREE tracking when you purchase the label online, Saturday delivery, and FREE **Carrier Pickup.** I utilize *Carrier Pickup* to have my mail carrier pick up my packages and scan them into the system immediately, meaning tracking is uploaded within an hour for both my customer and me; however, I must have at least one *Priority Mail* or *First Class* package to request a pickup. For example, if I have all Parcel Select packages, I cannot request this free pickup service (although at this point, I have such a good relationship with my postal carriers that they will gladly take any packages I have out). Since I work from home, *Carrier Pickup* is a blessing as I do not have to make multiple trips to the Post Office every week!

Of course, the best thing about *Priority Mail* is the FREE boxes! There are many sizes of *Priority Mail* boxes, including *Regular, Flat Rate*, and *Regional Rate* options, which I outlined in the first section of this book. And as I have also explained, their *Flat Rate Bubble Mailers* are extremely handy for shipping clothing and other soft items that weigh over one pound. If you are just starting out selling on Ebay, I recommend ordering 10-count packages of all the available boxes and envelopes (JUST the regular *Priority* and *Flat Rate* options, not the *Express* and *Overnight* versions) so that you will have an adequate supply on hand. Not only are the boxes FREE, but your postal carrier will deliver them right to your door for FREE, too.

TIP: Be sure to order plenty of boxes ahead of the busy holiday shopping season. By late summer, I try to stock up on all of the USPS Priority Mail boxes I will use between October and December. As the holidays get closer, the box supply shrinks, and they are much harder to come by. And while some Post Office locations carry a small supply of these boxes, most do not. If you need them in bulk, you'll need to order them online.

While the Post Office promotes their *Flat Rate* boxes and envelopes as having the best postage costs, regular *Priority Mail* is usually cheaper for packages less than four pounds. Why? Because when it comes to *Priority Mail*, it is not just the package's weight but also the distance a package has to travel.

As I mentioned previously, I live in Iowa. I can send a 2-pound package to Minnesota for a little over $7. However, that same package costs over $10 to ship to California. If that package is going to New York, the postage is around $9. To Hawaii or Alaska, the cost jumps to $13. Again, it is not just the weight, but the distance the package must travel.

The type of *Priority Mail* box (*Regular, Flat Rate,* or *Regional*) does not affect the speed of delivery, however. *Priority* is *Priority*. The shipping cost difference depends on the type and size of the box and the distance it will travel.

**Regular Priority Mail:** A regular *Priority Mail* box is priced by weight and the zip code to which it is being shipped. You can ship *Priority Mail* packages in regular boxes and envelopes, too, not only in the branded *Priority* boxes. The label that prints off from Ebay is branded as *Priority*. Still, we also keep *Priority Mail* stickers (again, FREE from the Post Office) on hand to ensure the package is easily spotted as *Priority* as the postal carriers do their initial package sorting. The stickers are also nice for covering up writing on boxes that we are repurposing.

The maximum weight for a *Priority Mail* package is 70-pounds. If you are using your own shipping box, note that the maximum combined length and girth are 108-inches, which means the combined measurement of the longest side and the distance around the package's thickest part cannot be more than 108-inches. A more straightforward calculation is not to use a box that measures larger than 12x12x12-inches. I keep a small supply of 14x14x14-inch and 16x16x16-inch boxes on hand, but I ship via *Parcel Select* or *UPS Ground* for those sizes. With increasing postage rates and limits on box sizes, these days, I try to stick to items that fit in 12x12x12-inch boxes or smaller, just to make my life easier!

As I mentioned, the Post Office provides FREE *Priority Mail* stickers to put on plain boxes and envelopes. I keep a roll of stickers on hand for when we ship *Priority* packages in plain boxes. But do not feel that you must use the stickers; the shipping labels are designated as *Priority*. The *Priority* stickers are just another shipping supply item we like to keep on hand.

**Flat Rate Priority Mail:** *Flat Rate* boxes have a set price. You can pack them up to 70-pounds and pay one flat rate no matter where the package is going. However, there are various sizes of *Flat Rate* boxes and envelopes, each with its own price. The Post Office is continuously raising prices, but as of this writing, the envelopes and small boxes start at around $7, the medium boxes ship for a bit over $14, and the large box ships for nearly $20. The price varies depending on whether you print the labels yourself on Ebay or at USPS.com (cheaper) or have the Post Office print them for you (more expensive).

While the Post Office heavily promotes *Flat Rate* boxes as the best option, *Flat Rate* is often more expensive than shipping via regular *Priority*. For instance, say you have a ceramic dish that weighs three pounds once it is in a shipping box. If you put it in a *Medium Flat Rate* box, it will cost over $14 to ship anywhere in the country. Now, if you are in Florida and your buyer is in California, that works out to be a great deal. However, if your buyer lives in your state or in a surrounding one, you could save as much as $7 in postage by choosing regular *Priority Mail.*

Again, by using Ebay's shipping tool, you will be able to see and compare all the options available so that you can find the best deal on postage for each order. However, note that if a customer pays for *Priority*, you need to ship the item *Priority*. *Priority* is an *Expedited Service* and is the fastest option as compared to *Media, First Class*, or *Parcel*. So, if your buyer pays for *Priority* but you downgrade them to *Parcel,* they are rightfully going to be angry.

**Regional Priority Mail:** *Regional Rate* boxes are a new offering from the Post Office. There are four different sizes available: **A1, A2, B1,** and **B2.** They also used to have a *C* option, but they have done away with those. I have found that the *A1* and *A2* boxes are often cheaper than the regular *Priority Mail* boxes for the shipments I do. I only keep the two sizes of the *A* boxes in stock as they are the only ones I use; I have not stocked the *B* boxes in months as I just never used them.

The downsides to *Regional Rate* are that the boxes themselves are on the smaller size and have lower weight limits (15 pounds for the A and 20 pounds for the B boxes). However, I keep a supply on hand in case I find that they are the best option. Again, since I ship via Ebay, I can look at all the shipping options before purchasing a label. As postage rates have increased, I have found myself reaching for the *Regional Rate A* boxes increasingly, mainly since I am currently focused on only selling smaller items.

**More About Priority Mail:** When packages are being sorted for shipment at the Post Office, the most expensive postage options go first as they are guaranteed space on the trucks and planes. *Overnight* and *Express* are obviously the most expensive since the customer is paying for 1-2-day delivery. *Media Mail* and *Bulk Mail* (bulk mail is usually "junk" mail that is sent out in mass) are the cheapest and, therefore, the last packages to be put out for delivery. It is all about available space; the more room on the truck or plane, the more packages they will ship out.

The Post Office promotes *Priority Mail* as being delivered in 2-3 business days. Again, that is BUSINESS days, i.e., WEEKDAYS. While some large postal facilities process mail on the weekends, the vast majority do not. Mail and packages are not processed on federal holidays, either. Ebay stands behind sellers in shipping times when it comes to mailing out orders on weekends and holidays; keep these rules in mind if you have a customer demanding that the order that they placed on Friday arrive by Monday. Unless your handling time is set as same day, you wouldn't have to ship that order until Monday.

After *Priority*, *First Class Mail* is the next class to be shipped out, followed by *Parcel Select*, and finally *Media Mail.* It is always in your best interest as a seller to use the fastest option available, depending on the price. The faster the customer receives their order, the happier they will be!

**International Shipping:** International shipping used to be such a massive headache that most sellers avoided it altogether. While you certainly do not need to ship to Canada, South America, or overseas, doing so will significantly increase your business. Fortunately, Ebay now offers its **Global Shipping Program**, an optional program you can opt into. Truth be told, Ebay will most likely put you into *Global Shipping* whether you opt-in or not. I specifically opted OUT of the program twice, only to be put back in it. However, now that I am enrolled, it has been smooth sailing, and I kick myself for waiting so long to opt-in.

When a seller offers international shipping and opts into the *Global Shipping Program,* their international packages are sent to a sorting facility here in the United States. So, when I get an international shipment notification through *Global Shipping,* the label that prints out and the postage paid is to a Kentucky facility. After the package arrives at that sorting facility, Ebay takes full responsibility for it, including filling out customs forms and putting on the postage to send to the buyer's country. Once a package reaches the Ebay facility, it is entirely in Ebay's hands, meaning if it is lost or if it arrives damaged, Ebay, not the seller, is responsible.

Because international shipping is now so easy using Ebay's *Global Shipping* program, there is no reason not to opt into it. Opening your sales to international customers will significantly increase your sales, and now printing a label is as easy as printing one for the United States.

However, some sellers still do prefer to ship internationally on their own. While I certainly do not recommend that new Ebay sellers who are struggling with shipping within the United States to try tackling international shipping, too, here are some essential points for those of you who at least want to know a bit more about how to ship your Ebay orders internationally if you are not using Ebay's *Global Shipping Program:*

- International orders ship via *First Class* (under 4 pounds) or *Priority* (four pounds or more)
- There are other services available, specifically *Express* and *Overnight*; however, in all my years of selling on Ebay, I have only ever had one international buyer re-

quest one of these faster services.

- While shipping a package via *First Class* to Canada may only cost a few dollars, most international shipments cost much more. Therefore, if you offer international shipping, you will want to make sure that the buyer is paying the postage cost to have the item delivered to their country.

- When you set up your domestic shipping, the same package weight and dimensions carry over to the international options; so, you only have to offer customers either *First Class* or *Priority*. Ebay's shipping calculator will figure out the postage cost based on the buyer's location. Let's say you are listing a coffee mug in the 1-2-pound range; you will offer *Parcel* or *Priority* for US customers and *First Class* or *Priority* for international customers. Ebay's *Shipping Calculator* will then do the rest.

- When you pay and print for your shipping labels through Ebay, the shipping label and the customs form to print out together. You simply sign the customs form and then attach both the label and the customs form to your package.

- If you do not print your labels but instead take your packages to the Post Office for postage, note that you will need to fill out the customs forms there. The form requirements change frequently, so you will need a postal clerk to give you the correct forms and explain how to fill them out. This is just another reason you should print your shipping labels out yourself at home!

- Due to customs regulations in other countries, some buyers will ask you to mark their orders as a "Gift" to avoid paying customs fees. Note that this is illegal to do and could result in being suspended from using USPS services; be sure to tell any buyer who asks you to do this that you cannot and will not. Always mark international orders as "Merchandise." If the buyer persists, you can put in a cancellation order through Ebay under the terms that the customer is asking you to violate a shipping policy.

Regardless of whether you ship international orders on your own or through Ebay's *Global Shipping* program, be aware that international packages' tracking varies greatly and is quite unreliable. More than the hassle of dealing with customs forms is the frustration of not always tracking international shipments. And without tracking, it is very easy for a customer to claim they never received their order, which means you will have to issue them a full refund. If you are shipping items on your own, you will ultimately be responsible for any lost or damaged packages. When you use Ebay's *Global Shipping,* however, Ebay is accountable for any shipping issues.

While Canada, the United Kingdom, and Australia all offer easy-to-track, generally reliable shipments, there are some areas of the world you may want to consider avoiding. Before I shipped through Ebay's *Global Shipping Program*, I blocked several countries and regions, including all of Central and South America, all of Africa, all of the Middle East, and Italy. While the other European countries offer fairly reliable shipping, Italy is notorious for holding packages up in customs and losing them. Mexico and the other South American counties also offer poor tracking, and shipping to anywhere in Africa or the Middle East is very risky as many online scams originate from those countries. The vast majority of international customers who buy from American Ebay sellers are in Canada, England, and Australia; for many years, those were the only areas I would sell to.

Once a shipment arrives in the country of the buyer, it first must go through customs. As I have mentioned, some countries do this very quickly, while others (Italy) are notoriously slow. International shipping can take as little as a week to arrive in Canada or up to a month or more for countries overseas. When I shipped internationally on my own, I was always dealing with messages from overseas buyers wanting to know where their packages were. But by using Ebay's *Global Shipping*, I never hear from international customers as Ebay handles any questions they have about their packages.

While shipping international packages outside of Ebay's *Global Shipping* program can offer cost savings to the customer as they do not pay both you AND Ebay for postage, the time and confusion for new sellers can be too much. Doesn't using Ebay's *Global Shipping Program* sound much better? It is so easy, and Ebay protects you from lost or damaged packages. I will never go back to shipping internationally on my own!

# PART THREE: HOW TO SET UP THE SHIPPING IN AN EBAY LISTING

For new Ebay sellers, the shipping section in the listing process is by far the most confusing. However, it is actually effortless once you understand how to set it up. And the best part is that once you set up the basic settings, they carry over to your next listings, meaning you only have to change a couple of settings for each new listing.

Now that you understand the basic four categories of USPS shipping options (*First Class, Media, Parcel,* and *Priority*), it is time to choose the ones you want to offer for your listings. One of the biggest mistakes new Ebay sellers make is trying to guess at shipping costs, resulting in either overcharging customers or undercharging them and losing money on shipping. However, as I discussed earlier in this book, using **Calculated Shipping** will protect you and your customers from incorrect postage costs.

I am a firm believer in using *Calculated Shipping* on Ebay for packages weighing over one pound. If you have a digital scale, there is no reason not to use it. *Calculated Shipping* means the buyer pays the exact shipping cost for the item's weight and for the zip code it is being shipped to.

While more seasoned Ebay sellers like to experiment with "free" shipping (i.e., building the shipping cost into the price of an item), I recommend you stick to *Calculated Shipping* when you are just starting out and have the buyer pay shipping. This will protect you from LOSING money by trying to guess shipping costs. It also ensures a fair shipping rate for the customer, which means you won't get angry customers who think they were overcharged for shipping. You can experiment with "free shipping" once you are more comfortable selling and shipping on Ebay.

So, you have a digital postage scale and are ready to create a listing using *Calculated Shipping*. It is so easy to do; here is how:

First, put your item into a box like the one it will ship it out in. Note that the box does not have to be the exact one you will end up shipping the item in; you just want a box close to the size and weight of the one you will be using. Boxes can quickly add up to one pound of weight to a shipment, so you need to get an idea of what box you will be using.

For example, if you are selling a coffee mug, place it in a 7x7x6-inch *Priority Mail* box or a similar sized box. Set the box on the digital scale and note the weight. Perhaps it comes out to 1-pound and 4-ounces.

So, in the Ebay listing under package weight, you put in 1-pound and 4-ounces, right? WRONG! When you are dealing with weights above a pound (remember, 16-ounces or less can go via *First Class*; and since the mug is not a book, it cannot go via *Media Mail*), you do NOT need to know the EXACT weight; you only need to know the RANGE between pounds. Understanding that you only need to know the RANGE will make your shipping process go much more smoothly.

If a mug in a box weighs 1-pound and 4-ounces, you simply select the 1-2-pound range under *Calculated Shipping*. You do NOT need the exact ounces. In fact, because the box will weigh MORE than 1-pound 4-ounces when it ships out (due to packing materials), that initial weight will not be accurate, anyway.

See how easy it is when you only need to know the weight RANGE? 1-2 pounds, 2-3 pounds, 3-4 pounds, etc. When an item is being shipped via *Parcel Select, Priority Mail,* or *Media Mail,* you only need to know the RANGE of weight. There is no need to worry about being exact down to the ounce!

I mentally add 3-ounces to all items I list to account for packing materials. Yes, packing paper, newspaper, bubble wrap, packing peanuts, enclosures, and tape will add additional weight to the shipment. So, for the mug in the box that weighs in at 1-pound and 4-ounces, I mentally note the weight as being 1-pound and 7-ounces. However, I still do not need to put in that exact weight. I only need to put in that it is 1-2 pounds.

Mentally adding in the packaging material weight is necessary for when packages are close to going to the next pound. For instance, say you have an item in its shipping box with a beginning weight (before packing materials) of 1-pound and 15-ounces. Obviously, when you add in packing materials, the weight will bump up to over 2-pounds and will need to be listed in the 2-3-pound range on Ebay. The same is true if the initial weight is, say, 2-pounds and 13-ounces. When you add in another 3-ounces for packing materials, the weight will be at 3-pounds and will need to be listed in the 3-4-pound range.

So, now that you understand about the shipping options and weights let's set up the **Shipping Details** in an Ebay listing!

The shipping section within an Ebay listing is located about three-quarters of the way down the page under *Shipping Details.* You will be selecting the shipping services first and adding the weight last.

The first section is for **Domestic Shipping.** The drop-down menu lets you choose from four options:

- **Flat: same cost to all buyers**
- **Calculated: cost varies by buyer location**

40

- **Freight: large items over 150 lbs.**
- **No shipping: Local pickup only**

Unless you are shipping a piece of furniture or only offering pickup, you will only need to select the **Flat** OR **Calculated** options before moving on to the next step.

Once you have chosen *Flat* or *Calculated*, you will need to select **Services**. This is where your digital scale comes into play. If you have a lightweight item weighing under one pound (don't forget to add in the 3-ounces for packing material), then you will be able to choose *USPS First Class Package (2 to 5 business days)*. However, you can also add in other options under that. I usually offer *USPS Priority Mail (1 to 3 business days)* for the second option. If you want to offer more than one shipping option, just click on *Offer additional service.*

Most of my orders are over 1-pound, so I always offer *USPS Parcel Select Ground (2 to 9 business days)* as my first option since it is promoted as an *Economy Service* and gives the impression that it is the cheapest option available to the buyers. I then offer *USPS Priority Mail (1 to 3 business days)* as the second option for buyers who want to choose an expedited shipping service.

As you will see, when you look at all the shipping options, there are a lot to choose from. I know that looking at all the choices is very overwhelming for new sellers; but just remember to focus on the four I have talked about, which on Ebay are listed:

- **USPS Media Mail (2-8 business days)**
- **USPS First Class Package (2 to 5 business days for packages a pound or less)**
- **USPS Parcel Select (2 to 9 business days for packages over a pound)**
- **USPS Priority Mail (1 to 3 business days for fast delivery of packages over a pound)**

While you may select other options such as *Flat Rate* or *Regional* when you print a label (more on this in the next section), you only need to offer your buyers any one of those options in the actual Ebay listing.

Note that you can choose to offer "Free shipping" on your items if you have made sure to build in the cost of shipping to the purchase price of your item. If you are selling a book that will ship via *Media Mail* for $4, you want to add that $4 to the book's cost. If you list the book for $5 with "free shipping" after the cost of postage and your Ebay fees, you will lose money.

The next choice you need to make is your **Handling time,** which is the number of days it will take you to ship the item after receiving cleared payment. As Ebay points out, buyers like to get their items fast, so I recommend that you choose a handling time between 1 and 3 days.

Because I work from home and utilize *Carrier Pickup*, I offer a handling time of *2 business days.* This means that I ship my items with two BUSINESS DAYS (i.e., weekday) after a buyer's payment clears. If a buyer pays for their item on a Tuesday, I will ship it out on Wednesday or Thursday. However, if they do not pay until Friday, their item will not ship until Monday.

The next section is for **International shipping.** I recommend just going with **Ebay's Global Shipping Program**, which means you will simply ship any sold items to Ebay's shipping center in Kentucky. From there, they will take care of all customs forms and assume responsibility for shipping the package internationally. Since you will be shipping the item to Ebay's US processing center, the buyer will pay the shipping charges offered under the "Domestic services."

Finally, you are now at the **Package weight & dimensions**, where you will put in the package's weight. First, Ebay has a **Package type** field where you can choose from four options:

- **Letter**

- **Large Envelope**
- **Package (or thick envelope)**
- **Large Package**

If you are selling small to mid-size items, you can simply select the **Package (or thick envelope)** option. That is the only option I ever choose. Remember that *Letter* and *Large Envelope* are for flat letter mail; any package, even if in a padded envelope, must go via *Package (or thick envelope)*. Unless you sell items such as stamps, postcards, or trading cards, your items will likely ship via *Package (or thick envelope)*.

Next is a field for the **Box dimensions.** Good news – you can completely skip this! The only time you would need to provide a box size up front is if you are shipping an unusually large item that is over 12x12x12-inches. You will need to add your box size when you print the item if it is shipping via *Parcel* or *Priority*. You never need to provide the box size for *Media* or *First Class*. Again, stick to boxes that are 12x12x12-inches or less, and you will be fine. If it makes you feel better, you can enter 12x12x12 into all of your listings if you aren't planning on shipping anything larger.

The last field to enter is **Weight**. If you are shipping something that weighs one pound or less, choose the first option, "1 lb. or less," and enter the ounces. **Here is a tip:** No matter how many ounces the package weighs, put in 16-ounces. Yes, it will slightly overcharge some packages; but just chalk up any additional funds to your handling fee. For items weighing a pound or more, simply select the range, as I talked about earlier. 1-2 pounds, 2-3 pounds, 3-4 pounds, etc.

Finally, you can **Exclude shipping locations**. Suppose you are shipping internationally on your own and not using Ebay's Global Shipping program. In that case, I strongly advise blocking buyers in some regions of the world prone to fraud and missing packages. Known trouble spots are all of Africa and the Middle East as well as Italy. Most international buyers on Ebay are from Canada, the

U.K., and Australia anyway, and they are all safe places to ship to. However, where to sell to is entirely up to you. If you are nervous about shipping internationally at all, even though *Global Shipping*, stick to domestic shipments until you feel more confident.

The next step to completing your is to click on the **List item** button at the bottom of the page, which will make your listing live and for sale on Ebay's site. However, you can first **Preview** the listing to see what it will look like when live; and you can also **Save as draft** if you still need to add some details to it.

After I submit a listing, I like to open it up to review what it actually looks like on the site. Sometimes I can quickly catch a mistake I may have made in the title or on a photo. I also utilize the "share" buttons located within each live Ebay listing to share it out to Facebook, Twitter, and Pinterest.

And that is it! Now that you have completed one Ebay listing with the shipping settings, the easiest way to create your second Ebay listing is to open the first and click on **Sell Similar**. *Sell Similar* will copy the first listing's information into a brand-new listing. From here, you just need to change the categories, titles, photos, item specifics, and description. Once you get to the shipping section, you will simply change the available package options and the weight, if applicable.

TIP: I recommend that when you are listing new items to Ebay that you list similar items back-to-back. This will cut down on the changes you need to make in each new listing. For instance, let's say you have ten shirts to list. All are under one pound, and you intend to charge buyers $4.99 shipping for each. After you have listed the first shirt with those shipping specifications, simply click on the *Sell Similar* option so you will not have to change the shipping settings in the second listing.

Or, perhaps you are listing several coffee mugs. You know that each will ship in the 1-2-pound range once they are packaged; so, in the first listing, you set up *Calculated Shipping* in the 1-2-pound range and offer both *Parcel Select* and *Priority Mail* for buyers to choose from. Ebay will automatically charge each customer to postage cost for their zip code. Once your first listing is live, open it up and click on *Sell Similar* to create a new listing. While you will need to change the title, photos, and item specifics, you will not have to change the shipping as it is identical to the first listing you created.

TIP: Often *Priority Mail* postage costs almost the same as *Parcel Select,* and sometimes it is even less depending on where the package is going. Most buyers will choose *Parcel Select* as it shows up as the "economy option" for them. However, if you can ship the item via *Priority* for around the same price AND put the item in a free *Priority Mail* box, you will not only save money on the packaging, but you will have a happy customer who receives their order much faster than had it shipped via *Parcel.*

I tend to build the cost of postage into the item cost so that I can offer "free shipping" to my buyers. Now, of course, there is no such thing as "free shipping" as someone, in this case, me as the seller, must pay for it. But if I offer "free" *Parcel* shipping for my buyers but almost always end up choosing *First Class* or *Priority* (depending on the weight) so that the buyer receives their item faster. Giving my customers this upgraded service costs them nothing, but they are almost always happy when their order arrives well before they expected it. And for me, if I can upgrade them to *Priority*, I can use one of the free *Priority Mail* boxes or envelopes provided by the Post Office (and delivered to me for FREE), which saves me the out-of-pocket expense of buying plain shipping boxes.

# PART FOUR: PRINTING SHIPPING LABELS THROUGH EBAY

So, you have boxes, packing materials, and a digital scale. You understand the four main USPS shipping categories (Media Mail, First Class Mail, Parcel Select, and Priority Mail). And you know how to set up the Calculated Shipping in your Ebay listings easily. You have sold an item, the buyer has paid, and now it is time to print the shipping label.

Once a customer pays for their item, Ebay will notify you that the buyer has paid and that it is time to ship the package. Depending on what your handling time determines how quickly you need to ship the item. I have my handling time set to two business days; note that business days means Monday through Friday, not Saturday or Sunday. However, I almost always print the shipping label within an hour of the customer paying and ship the package out the following day. Because I utilize the FREE Carrier Pickup service from the Post Office, I can ship out packages daily.

When you log into your Ebay account (I have mine bookmarked so that I am immediately directed to my **Seller Hub**), you will immediately see a notification that you have orders pending shipping. Once you access your **Seller Hub**, you will see this under

**Tasks.** Click on **Pending Shipments** to be taken directly to the orders that you need to ship. Here you will see all your orders that need to be shipped.

The default selection in the drop-down menu next to each of the orders that you need to ship will be to **Print Shipping Label.** All you need to do is click on that link, and you will be taken to Ebay's **Print your shipping label** screen. Please note that sometimes you may have to log in a second time here due to Ebay's tight security settings.

The Ebay label printing screen has **Print your shipping label** at the top, along with the **Order details.** Listed here will be the **Ship to address** for the buyer and the **Ship from/Return to (your) address.** You only must choose **Print format** once; Ebay will remember it for the next time you go to ship an order. I have my settings at *PDF 8" x 11"* as I print on two-to-a-sheet mailing labels. Here is where you can also preview what the shipping label will look like.

You will also see the item that sold, which is clickable and will take you to a copy of the listing. And you will see the buyer's Ebay user name, the shipping service they selected (or that you chose for them when you set up the listing), the order value, the delivery charge, and the expected date of delivery.

In the middle of the screen is the section called **Package.** This is where new Ebay sellers typically get tripped up, so take a breath as we go through it. I promise you; it is easy. After you have shipped out a few packages, I assure you that this will become a routine step for you in no time!

Since you set up your shipping preferences when you created your listing, the selections here will match those from the listing. Let's say you are shipping a women's blouse. When packaged inside of poly mailer, it weighs less than a pound, and you listed the shipping option as *USPS First Class* mail. That option will automatically be selected for you under the *Service* section of the page.

However, let's say that you offered *Flat Rate* shipping of $5.99 for the shirt, which the buyer paid. When you put the shirt into a poly mailer and weighed it, the weight came to ten-ounces. While you can ship via *First Class* for items 1-pound or less, the price differs by ounces. **The ounce parameters for First Class packages are:**

- **1-4 ounces**
- **5-8 ounces**
- **9-12 ounces**
- **13-16 ounces**

Your shirt can ship in the 9-12-ounce range, which means not only will the $5.99 shipping cost over your postage, it will also give you a bit of extra money to put towards shipping supplies. Think of these types of overages as your handling fee.

For the shirt, I would typically just type 12-ounces into the **Weight** field. Since the cost is the same in the 9-12 range, I do not have to enter the exact 10-ounce figure. However, the weight will show up on the label, so I like to put in the highest amount and account for any slight adjustments between my digital scale and the Post Office's.

Next to *Weight* is **Dimensions.** I usually leave this at the default of 1x1x1 until it is time to ship an item as I am never quite sure what envelope or box I will be using. However, unless you are shipping something larger than 12x12x12, you can put whatever dimensions you want here. Sometimes when I list an item, I will just enter 10x10x10, and that size will then show up on the shipping label page. The main point here is to show that you are shipping something that is UNDER what USPS considers oversized. If I were shipping something in a 14x14x14 box, I would need to put in those measurements as they would affect the package options and shipping costs available.

But, back to the shirt. You have changed the *Weight* to 12-ounces, you have left the *Dimensions* at their default of 1x1x1, and *USPS First Class Package* has been automatically selected under *Service*. There are some **Additional Options** available to you, including:

- Require Signature at delivery (use this only for items of high-value)
- Add additional liability coverage (this is added insurance; only buy this if your item is valued over $100)
- Contains hazardous materials (click on the link next to this option to see all the restricted items)
- Display postage value on the label (I make sure this is NOT checked so that the buyer does not see that they may have paid a bit more for shipping)
- Add custom text on the label (this is if you want to add an inventory number)
- Add a message in the dispatch confirmation email

I leave all these options unchecked. In fact, I rarely even notice them! Once if I am shipping an item that the buyer paid over $200 for, do I select *Require Signature*; and if I do, I always make sure to let the buyer know so that they will know that they will need to sign for the package.

Underneath these options is **Select how to pay**, and if you are in *Ebay's Managed Payments,* the cost of the label will be taken out of your pending payouts. If you have yet to be enrolled in Ebay's *Managed Payments* and are still utilizing PayPal, Ebay's system will automatically take you to PayPal to confirm payment of the shipping label. The system will then automatically return you to Ebay to complete the shipment.

Finally, you will see the total cost of postage next to the **big blue button titled Purchase and print label.** By clicking on that, your Ebay shipping label will print. Easy! After your shipping label prints, you will also be able to print a packing slip if you so desire. I always include a packing slip in my packages; it is not only a professional touch, but it also helps me stay organized as I have the packing slip with the shipping label so that I can double-check which box is shipping to which customer.

Let's go back and change the example of the item you have sold from a shirt to a coffee mug. While you listed the shirt with *Flat Rate Shipping* of $5.99, the coffee mug weighs over a pound when packaged in a shipping box. Therefore, you cannot send it via *USPS First Class*. In fact, the cost to ship the mug will vary widely depending on the buyer's location. I live in Iowa, and for packages over one pound that ship to California, the postage cost is nearly $11. However, the same package can ship to Minnesota for around $8. And with the Post Office continually raising the postage cost, the shipping charges keep going up and up. That is why it is so important to use *Calculated Shipping* on orders that weigh over one pound UNLESS the item can ship in a *Flat Rate* box.

As I covered earlier in this book, the USPS offers several sizes and types of *Priority Flat Rate* envelopes and boxes, including *Regional Rate* options. The most popular *Flat Rate* option for resellers is the *Priority Mail Flat Rate Bubble Mailer* as many non-breakable items, such as jackets and other bulky yet soft things, can be stuffed into the envelopes for a reasonable rate. The wide variety of shipping options is why I like to offer my customers the slowest, cheapest rate possible, and examine all the choices before paying for postage.

If you are using a *USPS Priority Mail FLAT RATE box*, select **Carrier packages** to choose which box or envelope you are using. You do not have to enter weight or dimension if you are shipping in a *Flat Rate* box or envelope, including *Regional Rate* boxes.

For instance, let's reexamine that coffee mug. You initially listed it in the 1-2-pound range with *Parcel Select* as the default option. Once you are in the *Print* your shipping label section, however, look at all the options available. Depending on where the buyer lives, the price could go up or down between *Parcel* and *Priority*, or you may see that using a *Flat Rate* box will be cheaper.

Let's say that you can ship the mug via *Priority* for the same or maybe even a little less than *Parcel.* That means you can ship the mug in a free *Priority Mail* box, and the buyer will get it faster than if it were going *Parcel Select*, and you may even profit a small handling fee if there is any excess. Plus, the customer will be happy that they received their order well before the promised delivery, which may result in them leaving you a five-star feedback rating.

However, you may find that *Parcel Select* IS the best price, so you can just stick with that; although unless the price is substantially more, I usually upgrade the package to *Priority* as I can use a free shipping box, and the customer will get their order faster. When you shop online, you get FREE tracking with *First Class, Parcel,* and *Priority* (*Media Mail* tracking has a small fee). You will also notice a discount on *First Class* and *Priority* shipping for printing the labels online. Free tracking and discount postage are two of the best reasons for shipping online through Ebay.

Once your shipping label prints, the postage and the fees associated with the sale will be taken from your Ebay pending balance account. If you are still using PayPal, the postage cost will be taken from your PayPal balance; but the fees associated with the sale will be added to your monthly Ebay invoice. The label's cost is paid directly to the USPS within Ebay's (or PayPal's) system. So, if you are enrolled in Ebay's *Managed Payments*, once the label is printed, all your Ebay fees and postage costs related to that order have been paid; you do not owe any more money to Ebay or USPS regarding that particular order. However, you will still have a charge on your account for your Ebay store subscription, if you have one.

Note that if you are not yet enrolled in *Managed Payments* and are still shipping through PayPal that all fees associated with your sales will still be billed to you every month via your Ebay monthly invoice. One of the benefits of using *Managed Payments* is that all fees, except for your monthly Ebay store subscription fee, are automatically taken out simultaneously as you print your shipping label. So, if you have not yet enrolled in *Managed Payments,* now is a great time to do so. Besides, Ebay will automatically enroll all sellers by 2022, so, in my opinion, it is best to enroll now so that you are not surprised by being suddenly enrolled. It can take about a week for Ebay to transfer your account from PayPal to their *Managed Payment system*, specifically because they will need to confirm your bank account to issue your payments.

As I mentioned, after you print your label, you also have the option of printing a packing slip. Simply click on **Open packing slip** if you would like to print one. I always include a packing slip in my orders, but not all sellers do. Again, the decision is yours to make.

**Packing Your Orders:** Once your label has been printed, both you and the buyer will receive notice from Ebay that the package has shipped. The tracking information will be included in this notice, and it will also be uploaded onto the item transaction page for both you and your buyer to access on your respective *My Ebay* pages. This is a wonderful feature as you, your customer, and Ebay now have confirmation from the USPS that the label has been printed. You do not have to type in tracking manually, and if there are any issues with a lost package, you will be able to show that you indeed did ship the item out within your stated handling time.

Now that you have your label printed, all that is left to do is package up your item and attach the label to it. Since you weighed the item in the box or envelope you planned to ship it in before you ever listed it, you will now want to go ahead and start packaging the item for shipment.

Even when selling used items and using secondhand packing materials, it is still essential to take time to package up your items in a clean and professional manner. As I discussed earlier in this book, I keep all sorts of packaging materials on hand, everything from recycled packing paper to bubble wrap. As you are just starting to sell on Ebay, try and use packing supplies from shipments you have gotten (you'd be surprised at how many of my Ebay orders ship in Amazon boxes!). If you do not have anything around, ask friends and family for any boxes, bubble wrap, and packing peanuts they may have.

If you are just going to sell on Ebay occasionally, you might be able to get most of your shipping supplies for free by reusing what you have or asking for people to give you their leftovers. However, it is crucial that whatever you use is CLEAN and from SMOKE-FREE HOMES! If you are a smoker, be sure to keep your inventory AND your packing supplies in an area away from the smoke. If your buyer detects even the slightest scent of cigarettes, they WILL complain!

Most clothing can be shipped in poly mailers or inside of boxes without any packing materials. However, hard goods will require a combination of packing paper, bubble wrap, and/or packing peanuts. You will want to carefully wrap the item and make sure it is surrounded by a buffer of packaging material in the box. I use newspapers to create a barrier around the item and the box sides, but I always make sure the item itself is wrapped in paper or bubble wrap away from the newsprint to prevent any print from rubbing off on the item.

If you are printing your shipping labels onto actual peel-and-stick labels, you will just need to remove the backing and stick the label to the package. However, if you are printing your labels onto paper, you will need to use clear packing tape to adhere the label to the outside of the box. It usually takes me three small pieces to cover the label and make sure it is stuck tightly. The only part of the label that I do NOT cover with tape is the bar code. You want to leave the bar code free of the tape so that the Post Office's scanning equipment can easily read it.

Once your label is affixed to your package, you are done, and the package is ready to be shipped out. If you are at home and can arrange for pickup, you will want to take advantage of the FREE *Carrier Pickup* service. If you have at least one *Priority Mail* or *First Class* package, your postal carrier will pick up all your packages for free. You do need to request package pick up the night before, however. You can request pickup online or through the USPS app. I have a large patio storage box on my front porch that I put my packages inside of; this protects them from the weather as well as potential thieves (yes, I have had packages stolen from my porch in the past). I have a small sign that I clip to my mailbox, letting the carrier know that packages are in the box. By now, all the carriers on my route know what I do and where exactly to look for the packages.

TIP: While you cannot give your mail carrier's cash, you can give them small gifts or gift cards valued at $10 or less. I give my primary mail carrier a $10 gift card every Christmas, usually to Starbucks or another local coffee place. I also put snacks out for all the delivery people during the holidays when they are dropping off and picking up many more packages from me than usual.

If you are not able to be home for *Carrier Pickup* and need to take your packages to the Post Office, note that you will likely have to stand in line and hand them to a clerk. Some Post Office's will make you wait while they weigh and scan in all your packages. If you end up shipping out many packages and develop a good relationship with the clerks, they may allow you to leave your packages on the counter. If you do hand your packages directly to a clerk, they can scan them and give you a receipt right there. I usually skip this since I have the tracking information from Ebay loaded onto my account.

And that is it! Your order is now in the hands of the Post Office and is on its way to the buyer. Ebay will notify the buyer that their order has shipped, providing both them and you with the tracking number. Both you and the buyer can then track the progress of the shipment. Note that the tracking numbers for each order are easily accessible next to the item itself in your *Seller Hub* list of orders that have shipped. Most buyers know how to access the tracking number, although new Ebay users may not. So, it is common for new buyers to ask you directly for the number.

The tracking numbers are essential to proving to Ebay that you did indeed ship an order should a buyer claim that they did not receive it. If a buyer opens a claim against you for an order not received, all you will need to do is provide them with the tracking number, which is easy to do as it was automatically included in the order's history.

One more tip about why I always try to upgrade my packages to *Priority Mail* even if the buyer agreed to Parcel Select: **Insurance**. Most *Priority Mail* packages are automatically insured up to $50. So, if a package is lost or damaged, either you or the buyer can submit a claim. In cases where an item arrives damaged, I issue the buyer a refund directly and then make the claim myself so as not to inconvenience them further. A quick internet search of *USPS Insurance & Extra Services* will take you directly to the page where you can file a claim for lost or damaged shipments.

# CONCLUSION

So that is it: Ebay Shipping Made Easy! I hope you have found this guide helpful as you embark on your Ebay journey. Selling on Ebay is fun and a great way to make extra money. For me and many others, it is a part-time or full-time business, one we can do from the comfort of our own homes. Please do not let any nervousness over shipping stand in your way. Ship your Ebay orders through Ebay at home, and enjoy having more time AND money from selling online!

Looking for more help with growing your Ebay business? Be sure to check out my other reselling books, all of which are available on Amazon on both Kindle and in paperback:

- BEGINNER'S GUIDE TO SELLING ON EBAY: https://amzn.to/34oFbX8
- EBAY SELLER SECRETS: https://amzn.to/3p6xKeT
- 101 ITEMS TO SELL ON EBAY: https://amzn.to/2Wqok1I
- 101 MORE ITEMS TO SELL ON EBAY: https://amzn.to/2LLIn8O

Check out my reselling planners and journals:

- 2021 RESELLER PLANNER & ACCOUNTING LEDGER: https://amzn.to/3nzHMoE
- 2021 RESELLER MILEAGE LOG BOOK & PLANNER: https://amzn.to/2WDx70x

- MY RESELLER STORY GUIDED JOURNAL: https://amzn.to/3nw0jCm

Interested in starting a YouTube channel? Check out my book:

- HOW TO START A YOUTUBE CHANNEL FOR FUN & PROFIT: https://amzn.to/2KftrPN

# ABOUT THE AUTHOR

Ann Eckhart is a writer, reseller, and online content creator based in Iowa. She has numerous books available about how to make money online and from home. Check out her Amazon Author Page at https://amzn.to/34nE9us for all her titles.

You can keep up with everything Ann does on her blog at www.AnnEckhart.com. You can also connect with her on the following social media networks:

FACEBOOK: https://www.facebook.com/anneckhart/

TWITTER: https://twitter.com/ann_eckhart

INSTAGRAM: https://www.instagram.com/ann_eckhart/

YOUTUBE RESELLING CHANNEL: https://tinyurl.com/yxvqtwc7

YOUTUBE VLOG CHANNEL: https://tinyurl.com/yxjqn6d2

Made in the USA
Columbia, SC
23 June 2024

37418990R00036